CW00956470

PLANET-STR

ALSO BY JULIAN TURNER

Crossing the Outskirts
(2002)

Orphan Sites
(2006)

Julian Turner
Planet-Struck

ANVIL PRESS POETRY

Published in 2011
by Anvil Press Poetry Ltd
Neptune House 70 Royal Hill London SE10 8RF
www.anvilpresspoetry.com

This book is published with financial assistance
from Arts Council England

Designed and set in Monotype Dante by Anvil
Printed and bound in Great Britain
by Hobbs the Printers Ltd

ISBN 978 0 85646 435 5

A catalogue record for this book
is available from the British Library

DUM SPIRO SPERO

While I breathe I hope

ACKNOWLEDGEMENTS

Acknowledgements are due to the following, where some of these poems first appeared:

Poetry London: 'Fools', 'The Yoredale Beds', 'In the Attic at Work'
Pennine Platform: 'Appletreewick'
Stand: 'Pastoral', 'At the Pagan Sites'
The New Humanist: 'A Nightjar'
www.bowwowshop.com: 'Craven', 'Elephant's Foot'

'The Eyes that Talk to the Sky' was written to be set to music by Aled Start for the 2009 Greenwich Early Music Festival.

Contents

Planet-Struck

At the Pagan Sites

My father showed me how to haunt such sites:
he disappeared as I walked after him,
returned to me as one small speck within

the larger field, wearing the clothes of sky,
his wet shirt flapping scarecrow-like, a kind
of corposant appearing to illume

the flake-white of his cheeks as if he came
back from a lonely lake on the far shores;
and in between the time he disappeared

and he returned, beside some nameless mound
I'd wait and watch the dark grow in the east,
a high wind fill the distant copse or pick

among the scraps and fents left in the ditch
for old time's cloth of gold and muddy gems.
Rustlings would follow him like after-steps.

They followed us when he would take a hold
of my hand, as silently he walked me back
to the thoughtless world of ordinary things.

We all spend some time there. I get away
as much as possible. I drive at dusk
and wait alone where lane-ends swing the lead.

Fools

"Bards are a malicious and untrustworthy set of people"
GIRALDUS CAMBRENSIS

To all petty chapmen and pedlars
    who wander abroad lodging in ale houses,
all fencers, bearwards and common players
    of enterludes and minstrels,
to all wodewoses, mendicants and peregrini,
    madmen, jugglers, gleemen, buffoons,
to all beggars and to those exposing their wounds
    for coin, all rhymers and their ilk,

understand that what you share in common
    is greater than the Acts of Vagrancy:
you are indeed the well from which
    the water of the gods is sourced,
the sacred spring from which all humankind
    would drink – the art of foolishness –
intense, unreasoned, the words arose in him
    and came forth in an unsightly flood

no one could understand: folly, poetry
    and saintliness lie under the one blanket,
the refuse of the Earth, the witless and the mill-
    horse are both as one thing,
the possession of deformity considered in itself
    safeguard against malignant influence,
the fool's mouth guarantee of fortunate success,
    the power of dream and prophecy in ecstasy.

You feathered Gelts – put on your cloaks
          and dance the god, chirrup like birds,
describe the place ten leagues beyond man's life,
          the shadowlands inhabited by ghosts
and speaking serpents; lost souls who court
          vituperation so as to obtain good luck,
sing of the overlooked and laughed at, sing
          into this world protection from the evil eye,

sing the clairvoyance of your calling, who walk
          asleep proclaiming the absurd, unbound;
sing for the imbecile and idiot, the men
          so far ahead that they have met themselves
on their return and quizzed the grizzled souls
          about the afterlife, the happy hunting ground.
Spirits who refuse to keep silent, unstop
          the bottle of your voice and pour out its salve.

Ceallunaigh

These half-hatched souls inhabit no-where-land –
a turfed mound enclosed by walls where bumps
stand for the un-memorialised, without a stone,
where tormentil opens its face towards the sun.

Under an uncomplaining sky they breathe
the turf, the warm air at the turf's root.
Their nutrients keep the pasture green all year
in this unmarked site beside a country road,

home to the stoat escaping from my feet;
to the mole, casting up its signs, which keeps
company with the bodies down below,
conversation where the unwanted sleep

in the unshorn hair of grass, all higgledy
and dewy in the morning sun. A wren
in clover on a cold and un-carved stone,
pouring out the liquid of its song.

Virtue

for Jacqui Dillon

The torturer looks down and sees the child.
The freckled hands adjust the bruising rope.
She hangs by one wrist over bottomless
abysses and his face fills her with hope.

Jet Stream

The glass has dropped: in youth I heard this phrase
and knew it meant days of incarceration,
the windows pitted by south-westerlies
as brine broke on the bungalow. We'd read
all day and dash into the waves at dusk –

those tortured, wrought-iron whorls of waves
which crushed and sucked the shingle into spheres
and turned our bodies blue – all propelled
by you from somewhere far off, the turbine
engine of air, the mother of all winds:

of Mezzar-ifoullousen, Mistral, Williwaw,
of black-winged Kuraburan blasts that blew
in Genghis Khan to torch our cottages,
of easterlies from Kiev which gave birth
to tumours from the cracked sarcophagus.

I feel a fondness for you, going about your business
in the ether-world of the atmosphere, because
you take the place of God, His thoughtful presence,
an abstract, invisible hand with agency
that moves things round in ways we can explain.

Tonight the ear-popping cyclonic gusts
shriek across Yorkshire like the Wild Hunt,
Gabriel Ratchet's Hounds which shred the sky,
whose sheer percussive tread flattens the oaks –
one glimpse of which informs you: you will die.

Ice

When I recall my father in the hospital morgue,
all of his features stilted, cold and a slight bloom
risen to his cheeks, each time I think of him
shaking with laughter, small, beady eyes squeezed
shut but with that sparkle in them clear as frost.

Codeine

I can remember when my ribs were knitting back
their splintered ends, the bone fusing between them

in secret. Then I used to walk gently for miles,
thinking how each step contributed to recovery

and I was gentle with myself enjoying the day
as it tailed off too early, listening to a wren

on a bare branch at dusk, or standing at our back door
breathing in the first scent of spring, a pleasant ache.

Lao's Mirror

The night sky rippling with aurora light,
the warm Earth making circles of the stars
and a hard frost clouding the eye of ponds.

Shaken from sleep beside the telephone
I drove all night, arriving before dawn
where willows had always waited by the beck.

I wanted to arrive before he died
and failed: long hours of alternating sodium
and sheer green dark had seemed to stretch my mind

so when I stop in that pause before morning
I'm sick of pain, as if I've left behind
my enemies who are not yet awake.

I am nowhere and have no name. I sneak
silently in and breathe quietly a moment
before undressing in front of the mirror

which speaks in gold devices and machines
whose feather touch can profile molecules
of soul amongst the early settlements.

The Extraordinary Rendition

Good, very good, this captures the enormity
of the acts. A catalogue of each machine
invented, implemented, used too well.
They've put them on the walls: the wheel, the branks,
the brazen bull, the pear of anguish, foot-screw
and heretic's fork, restored to working order.
One half expects, in a busy room behind
the snuggery, a franchised rental concern.

The Exhibits of Extreme Anger

Outside the Court the white van blanks their stares.
They show their teeth and throw their hands up high,
they scream and curse his vile and heinous ways.
The veins bulge on their necks – press them and see
the blood refill – small specks of spittle fall,
each fibre of their flesh wound clock-spring tight.
Look how the jowls shake and the lips reveal
the white lines of the underlying skull.
The exhibition indicates we're right
to blame this other for his blackened heart
because, curled round our coloured muscles, are
all monsters that we nurture with our thought.

Wraith Ferry

The Giant Hrim is at the helm,
his head half snagged; his fetid beard
drips on his boils. Fenris Wolf

howls on the deck, its spit-white jaw
stretching itself to swallow the sun.
The Ship sails on over the World-

Tree drowning in the turbid waste.
The sky splits open: fire and venom
spill out. Nothing is without fear.

The Ship is made from dead men's nails.
They grow on after death has come,
they grow in the dark grave, on the man

waiting to burn in his wood coffin,
they grow unstoppably. And you
who flick your parings at the bin

or stand and bite your finger ends,
remember every time you spit
you bring forward the Reckoning Day.

If you value a long life, pay
no attention to how much fruit
you eat, smoke whatever you want,

just make sure you burn your nails
because each paring builds towards
the launch of pale Naglfar

when Odin rides to Mimir's well;
God fights God and great chiefs suffer.
The rafters of the sky will burn.

The Yoredale Beds

My ear against the turf, I try
to hear my heart
sound underground, an echo of
a darkened sun.

An old wall lies below the grass
just to the north
of where the monks' road makes its big
sweep across Mossdale.

It runs below more recent walls –
shown only
as a shadow thrown by a low sun
and bears no name

on maps in this over-mapped land –
so old all trace
of cause or maker has long gone;
although close by

I see the marks of bronze-age men,
their villages lumps
in uneven fields beside the karst
where lapwings wheel.

Water has abandoned it
for the deep runnels,
unheard below the light green fleece
of the dry ground.

In the Black Keld hydrology
a violent storm
sent the flood pulsing through
the Marathon Crawls.

Under a great weight of rock
the shallow caverns,
carved by the water's patience, filled
to the ceiling in seconds.

Six bodies lie in the Mossdale caves
upslope from here,
the secret fruit of the earth we seek
on our brief journeys.

Bagot's Walking Stick

Charred and gaunt, it sticks up through a hedgerow
in my mind, a grand, aged oak, stark and blasted
by lightning, its huge girth part hollow now,

its black silhouette always beyond the last stead
on the lane to the sticks. As kids we used to trek
the county roads in search of it to picnic

at the altar of its trunk although we may
never have reached it, always stopping on
the way beneath some noon alternative.

Most of my life feels made of similar stays,
the chance halts by the road I'm travelling on
to some forked, splintered end I have to live.

Malham Cove

for PJR

Now that I have the vantage of the hill
to contemplate my old itinerary,
I am grateful that I have the wider view
and can take in each field and ruined mill,
each twist the path took on the lucky way
and how the pattern of it points to you;

now that the illness has already stripped
all trace of spring shoots from the spectacle,
helping me better see the shape of love
that lies behind the summers' leafy script,
and words and wishes wither as they fall
exposing what is simple, or enough.

The Eyes that Talk to the Sky

(Mata-ki-Te-rangi)

As the world opened up to
        endeavour and discovery,
our aperture widening until
        our view became infinite,

the painter saw it all unscathed –
        the stone sentinels aloof,
their backs turned to the sea,
        the sky resting on their shoulders.

Four bone fingers point against
        a glowering Pacific storm,
wind stood still in sunlight,
        presaging the echo boats

already approaching the horizon
        with their deaths and wreckage,
the stone spirits standing apart
        their proud heads high.

Cargo Cult

We live in the Hall of Mirrors, even here.
This morning I played my part, paring the ground
for the planned airstrip that will await the drop,
the parachutes I picture blooming above
our island paradise and the great weight
of commodities that will silently descend.

The goods the natives talk about are not
what will arrive. I believe that they expect
munitions, tobacco, uniforms and envelopes
of dollars they will burn with spice in the clearings.
I think like a man who can see his own shape
approaching him out of the jungle night.

As I cleared the ground of roots with my men,
sowing the compacted surface with its screed
of concrete, I caught sight of the men who slice
their arms with blades and rub their skin with ash,
far-off figures doing their dance, falling
over themselves in their delirium

to bring ships to the harbour, helicopters down.
The natives say independence is their only goal
but we know better: they long to become like us
who glow within ghost-white and feed ourselves
on manna which improves our flesh. Refreshed,
we smell of kindness. They say we smell of death.

Altiplano

to Olivia Harris

Now that you're dead I'll never live to see
that country in your head you showed to us
of miners, farmers and those who walk the lake,

their feet touching the blue with white splashes
on the icy surface, who are born and die on water,
who build their rafts from Totoro reeds and dwell

so high the blood that gives them life is black.
You walked with them, their llama caravans
winding down to where they lit their fires

from pure joy, the brush-wood being plentiful.
You taught us how to see the common thread
woven into the cloth that clad us all,

how all folk everywhere will snigger at
the powerful and how the ones who tread
the ziggurat of turquoise ice which climbs

sheer into the sky – where the gods toy
with the frozen children's curls, special delivery
they take delight in – are shod with snow and sing

to those cruel, cloud-torn giants up above
about the terraced gardens where they grow
the ordinary ornaments of life;

that world you conjured so that our poor minds
could glow, back in the bed-sits, with an Amerindian
nimbus, the place where breath and soul are one.

Hunters and Gatherers of the Twentieth Century

wormed their way into the distrustful hearts of those they shot
to catch the moment of unguarded mirth before the slap of fate;
showed how hope, that great illusion shouldered by the young,
adheres to sandals in the sun or any joyride impulse of the gang;
stopped down the speed of light to make the backdrop into blur,
fore-grounded faces which made you see what light was for,
raindrops glistening on the veranda shook by a passing boxcar;
called to a halt mid-gesture the shift from laughter to anger,
every gesture vulnerable, each look a portal to a haunted soul
and illustrated how the only truth of permanence is temporal.

Hibernaculum

Like my ancestors, who used to bring
the animals back down to the shore in winter,
abandoning the pastures of the sheiling
for more temperate machair,

I go downwards into my dwelling's bowels,
to the cellar library, there to spark
a stove. I stoke it full of wood and coals
and wrap myself in books.

Cadaver Dogs

for Timothy Taylor

The dogs have led their handlers to the site
and faithfully revealed the evidence:
whatever it is they find they bring to light.
They trace the truth by following the scents.

They find the corpses in the earthquake zones,
search for abducted children in the shires,
the disappeared and mutilated ones,
for extra arms and legs in funeral pyres.

They can discover decomposing flesh
in running water or below the soil,
they look for bodies in the children's crèche,
below the patio, in midden spoil:

the bits of gristle spat out on the ground,
blood from the beating heart, coagulate
and clot, the lymph and serum of a wound,
the smallest signature of DNA.

Awestruck and disbelieving, we look on.
Our feelings seethe below our skins or boil
as outrage shouted at these evil men,
our opposites, not getting it at all.

Homo Amnesiens, not long ago
we ate each other; not surprising then
we are experts in techniques to vex the soul,
to leave it stuck beyond the reach of men:

repeated rape and drowning to the point
of loss of consciousness confuse the brain
until it is disordered and disjoint,
uncertain how it can escape the pain.

Cadaver dogs bring back the buried dead.
They'll find us too, spread-eagled on red snow.
They fetch the bits back from the land ahead.
They will not let us say we do not know.

Memento

You say – *You bought that sea-horse mug for me*
on Broadway Market. Here it sits, its sand-
worn matt glaze undeniable as stone.

The market stands out in my memory
but when I search it for the stall, the stand,
the mug, all trace of buying it has gone.

Equinoctial

When the season's tipping point is reached
and winds begin to blow,
the nights grow longer than the days
and cast their own shadow,

when the whole wood groans and ash boughs smash
onto the leaves below
and hooves leave smoking imprints on
unseasonable snow,

when the season tips to chaos and
the cold begins to grow,
and the corpses on the street-lights swing
madly to and fro;

should we not picture the Wild Hunt
crashing across the gorse,
its limber wheels and wrecking crew,
its dogs and sumpter horse?

Henge and Cursus

Thornborough

On the flat floodplains of Mowbray, where the first settlers
carved their kinship into the coarse land, by the throat
of all rivers which revivify the plains, revealed between
the farthest sightings as a sea of silt, there they placed a
    choker;

this was the first man mark to make the meadows sweet,
at the hub they held in most high esteem and here they built
the great rivers the gods look gladly on, Wharfe and Swale,
Ure and Aire, here they sought to draw down the deluges

from the watershed to wash the wheat to serve them
and sought to helve the land to make it sing the song
of the svelte corn, the thorn song of the silver waterway,
here they drew designs on the dark land that nature knew

and matched them with their own myths to make sure
the waters would renew the soil with sand and silt,
for they had proved the power by pointing to the hills,
by calling flood to feed the crops and they could feel

the sureness circulating in their blood, in spirals,
bright loops of beauty so they knew themselves as blessed
and fixed the path by setting stones to keep the power pure,
draining from the high dales down to the plains, drawing

the path the flood would follow, fixing the foot of the sky
to the hills' rims so they could ladder up the horizon to
    hoist
their name into the sky in darkness, stitching the stars
to the ground, laying rivers on the land to make it leaf,

matching the lines the moon makes as it sails the sky,
white meadowsweet or other mortuary fronds, like
    moons
in mother dark, dreaming the darn that sows the earth
and sky and letting it mature in the mind like little loaves,

second-guessing the gods that groan in the thunderplump
or in the wail the winds bring with the western gales,
allowing themselves to dare to dream their dreams
of ruling boldly like them; but richer, better reigns.

Old Roads

The sun in threadbare brakes
where the trees hiss together;
on the banks of circling mottes,
the round shoulders of dreams
stir in the old earthworks
and generations which have gone
huddle closer for warmth.

What can I hear in the wind?
Surely it's not the jaggers,
drovers or husbandmen
walking along the old roads
in sunken lanes below
the surface of the present world,
calling out cold "amens",

nor is it the older deities
whose voices are the bass
that can only be half heard,
the deeper sounds that thrum
as autumn gold decays
replacing the drone and hum
of strimmer and honeybee?

Thorns pluck at my coat
like witch fingers: some hedge
spirit, envious and angry
at me, descending through
her memories like bone
splinters scattered in soil.
I hear the forgotten ones

who haunt the hilltop forts,
the rings and standing stones,
the lonely, barrow-walking
ones whose dry feet tread
the air above the falling leaves,
the turf maze built as both
palace and prison for the dead.

DIY Manual

Like most of them, it's practical:
you have to change the locks, alarm
the house, mount one of those fish-eye
video sentry surveillance stations
to cover all the entrances.

Ensure all incidents are reported:
it does not matter that they are not
investigated. Always act
as if protection was your right.
Get a good lawyer: keep her informed.

Operate through networks unfamiliar
to *Yellow Pages*. Do not trust
anyone you have not known for *years*.
Go out for walks to talk about
the issues. Keep a rein on your fears.

It is hard knowing you cannot speak
your part, nor answer allegations;
that you will never be believed
despite the clarity of what you know:
strong outlines keeping you awake.

Understand that working alone
is useful in itself: the fewer involved,
the less the risk, and solitude
brings its own rewards, like pride
which soon surfaces with a chuckle.

Above all, try to guard your charge.
Do it silently, secretly, with
conviction, courage, stamina.
Assume Inquiries cannot grasp
the truth. Keep it close to your heart.

Appletreewick

Everywhere the water's height
surprises, a great smooth swelling
over weirs, a sheer glass welling
above the banks as skeins of light
wind around themselves in mauves
and greys, the bearded islets broken
from the shores by the red churn
chafed with the white of rock-cleaved waves,
as if it had transformed the soft
rise of the ground to liquid, the scuff
of pasture rippling on the bones
of rock like shot silk, while the rafts
of farms, roped to their mooring stones
by walls, ride on a tide of turf.

The Forget-Me-Not Clock

Chevin: from the Welsh *cefn* meaning ridge,
it has been my own horizon for thirteen years
and I'm almost content to have my feet on it:
I've climbed it every day through the hard winter
when sleet stung my face and wind my bitter mouth,
climbed it in pain and fearfully to know
how feelings change the lie of branch and scarp,
how they alter the lichen look on a north-facing wall;
I've climbed up here in sun and at night when light
stored under leaves is slowly exhaled to lamp
the lonely traveller towards a door,
and I've stood still on a still grey day to hear
the drop of beech nuts through the leaves, a weird
and eerie 3D echo-sounding rain
and I have been the bride as autumn fell
on my head from russet to vermilion,
copper and bronze coins burying my boots,
the piles of wealth ignored and I have climbed
the ridge too worried to notice the fly agaric's
vivid red slash stashed underneath the bracken,
scared others might notice the monster in me
and shriek and point; I have strode along paths
or dawdled, stood and stared as the fields flicker
in the ever-changing light and I have climbed
in drumming rain when the ground goes liquid
and pours between the roots of ash; I've climbed
too in the thick snow and as the snow fell
and a silence with it as if I walked in cotton
wool and was sleeping-bagged in a warm glow.

* * * *

The wish for spring can be a form of hunger –
drinking the scents I understood the want,
wild and aboriginal – the loss of light
for five dark months can make the body thrum
like metal for it in the slow stretch of days
and yearn for blossom foaming on the sky,
for sun through freshly green or birdsong in
a re-embirded world, its colour back.
This healing came upon me on the hill:
the sun was reddening the west and slow
leaves were unfolding hands from sticky fists;
the mercy of the wind was drying them.
All day the great halls underneath the beeches
had boomed to a spring gale, groans from the boughs
a creaking like the whole world was a boat,
and the canopy had inhaled its vast lung
to power the sails of trees and turn the Earth,
but now the agony was spent and day
allowed the darkness to let out the light.
Although I know that this is not my land
under an ancient name, belonging elsewhere,
whose odd displacement is a home for me,
I felt a new warmth and the forget-me-not
clock was striking blue, the clouds were islands
in an estuary, the beeches leant together
whispering with their new softness of leaf,
stirred and aroused by a combing hand of wind,
the whole ridge seemed alive. It breathed and sighed
like a sleeping horse, moving, glowing with heat.

Pastoral

The farms here cast a deep shadow. A crow
sewing a corpse with the thread of sinew,
pulling it tight. It is surprising how

fit they are for a life among abandoned barns,
black clots like blood congealed in moon-
light, squatting in buttercup constellations,

flung up as inverted crosses against the sun
or quarrelling on silage-tyres. A bone
by the verge with torn wrappers, cellophane

and a single shoe which seems innocent.
Not what I'm meant to think, a revenant
sensation from a time to which I can't

return. The metal shutters clatter to.
Crows fidget in the roof space. Cattle low.

Never Finds the Day

I can no longer leave my house for fear
that if I do some visitor will call
passing through doors, possessing keys that give
him easy access where my darlings lie,
lifting duvets with in-taken breath,
and mark them with his passing so they die,
the beds becoming empty coops, the doves
flown off, leaving just rib-cages with blood
and scabs, the house's walls graffiti-daubed
with excrement and outpourings of hate,
each of our many simple acts of love
written over, cancelled out, like rain
blotting one whole side of a valley out
and I will never call it home again.

from The Arcades Project

Les Hirondelles

The picture frame which shows the items off
itself is gold, the chairs mahogany,
the auburn candle flames glow mutedly
like love-shot eyes and Bordeaux leather shines
behind the merchandise which wears the fee –

it all must be ablaze with soft gas-lilt,
all colours, radiant, from many ports –
everything glitters, ormolu and gilt,
the *produce which the common earth has built,*
gifts of the World from every quarter bought

and boated to this windowpane. They seem
as in their bedroom and at home, the sheen
of skin, duck eggshell of meringue or crème
brûlée, all paint and food, an in-between
confection, strange / familiar, a dream

you've had before, the bit of skirt you'd die
to get between the sheets, the petticoat
you would disrobe, but not too strange to lie
with in the semi-dark, so what you bought
is real enough to pinch, and money buys

a lot these days: behind the lightest touch
the slightest stroking of the cheek, its presence
can be felt, a ghost not here as such
but pulling strings, controlling each response
so you will dance, a puppet to its twitch,

the very picture of success and love,
their trappings and their surfaces, the look
of beauty, raven hair, that sort of stuff,
the kind of breathless shape Odysseus took
when laying Circe is what I'm thinking of –

these are transactions traded every day
but capital is blind and can't explain
what else exchanges hide: the secret way
to dump your shame by laying down a coin,
covering it with guilt, grief, dismay.

Who cares about the morality of these legs?
What one wants is to go where they go.
Shrug it off. For the night is young and begs
you let her go but you do not want to.
You want to see her bleed, the wasted hag.

Such souls of the night can never be made pure –
they'll shipwreck those who try to rescue them –
a kind of suburb of the mind where whores
haunt the industrial estates like dirty gems
and drape their arses on the rusting bars;

did you know how young they start them now?
Under the sodium in negligées
the children stand by cars, their mouths blasé
like pomegranates from the work of Poe,
and close them on the fountains of decay.

As young as four in our industrial towns
(not on display but in the catalogue)
they stand in line because the pimps and crones
who sell them beat them purple in the fog
and silence them with phenobarbitones.

The traffic like the great ocean conveyor
runs around the Earth and spreads the wares
to named, discriminating connoisseurs
and this is truly what they say they are,
rare experts of the most exquisite pleasures.

Elephant's Foot

This place of most uncertain status is a home for wolves,
beavers, polecats, racoon dogs, moose, boars, badgers,
lynx, Przewalski's horses, brown bears and deer of many
kinds.

The sun shines forever in the forests of The Zone, so bright
it makes me want to sneeze. The Upper Swamps have been
re-flooded
and are home now to a thousand black egrets. It is a miracle.

Of course, the elephant's foot, that globular mass formed
by the melted reactor core when it cooled just above
the water table, together with about two hundred tons

of nuclear fuel and fission products which exploded,
burned, melted and poured into the nooks and crannies
of the demolished reactor building and whatever else

is encased in the cracked, unstable sarcophagus, all
these are still so radioactive no one can currently
get close enough to study them and what they plan to do.

The forests whistle in an unplanned wind, the reeds
that orchestrate the world we are not present to observe.
A gate-post, rusting, plays a minor note as tree trunks fall.

Make Me Clean

Bleach burns can turn a jet skin to a white
patchwork of pools of paleness on the black;
like ceremonial cuts across the cheek
such signs can quarantine and set apart.

They vary from the carefully incised
lattice-work of scars that climb the arm,
to turbulent and stormy clouds of harm
dug into flesh and levered, twisted, prised.

Such marks are not exactly what they mean,
rather insignia which show the flaws
that might exist yet still disguise their cause:
no bleach is strong enough to make me clean.

Nothing New

for LS

Born to this strange town late in my life
I walk in the afternoon as lights come on
not recognising a landmark, neither the fish-
back of the Chevin nor the fascia
of outlets on this side of town, the back

side of the one I usually look upon, wondering
what I must have done to wash up here
in bland surroundings I forget each day,
which never seem new but only strange, like any
pavement anywhere; the light's the thing

decaying from dull to dusk, solid pieces
of it dropping off like ice in thaw and sealing
over tight with gaps where things should be
and if I try remembering what went before
the day opened in thick, grey blankets of rain

I'm left perturbed: as if a sudden swirl
in water was all that remained, its cause obscure
like the after-taste of fear, lingering and nothing
comes back, ever, although like you I end
my day asleep or out on foot, trying

to cheat forgetfulness by not allowing night,
by linking up what cannot be connected –
my body changing shape in front of me
as I stand before the mirror; treading on
the water of the Wharfe, testing its strength,

going in; my voices insisting I admit
my vices, many as they are. I have to mourn
the loss of everything and not know what
that is: town, country, lights, faces, hope
of tomorrow which is only ever thus.

Ghosts

Good for nothing, they sit around the fire
they cannot feel and with their feather touch
try to pry the angle of the intersect
between the worlds to find the way back in.
Companions and conspirators, they fray

at the edges of our sight and shift like smoke
and when we look they are not there; they stir
air circles in a medium that is not theirs;
the edge is their domain but how they long
for a body that will thrill to their control,

how they want the levers under their hands.
We know that nothing seems as good as flesh,
that coarse, flawed substance always cracking up,
which is water and as full of change, the filmy
medium we do our doings through. We know

they want to get to grips with ours and so
protect ourselves with whatever comes to hand
as if they were at our shoulder or behind
the ear, listening in to our bodily operations,
waiting their chance. From where I sit I watch

them materialise out of the grey light like clods
that will not stay still, crackling in lamplight,
washing me with their gaze, and those I can't
perceive, drifting up the blackened lane,
mouths open. To keep control I name their names:

doppelgänger, fetch and night gaunt, grave-
yard spectre, banshee, poltergeist and wraith,
crisis apparition, gytrash, earthbound phantom,
revenant and species of the other world.
Mistletoe and bell, candle, cross and charm.

Craven

To appreciate the deteriorated
crenellations of limestone,
their stepped terraces often hidden
below turf and the vanishing
of streams because such beauty
should be brought to mind often.

To love watching the water well
up in the meadows of pale green
where, from a standing start, the flow
building to a river in five yards,
a sudden generosity
of wetness its own reward.

The grass sings. To be overcome
when walking on a limestone pavement
with hart's tongue, herb Robert and
dog's mercury peeping from the dark
recesses of a grike together
with buried promises of light.

Remarkable the sunlit thorn
beside the white ribbon of a wall
casting its shadow on the plain
of fractured rock and juniper
crowding the dry ground, the road
hedgeless, the tarmac taped to grass.

And high up in this perfect space
on deep grey sword-wings, peregrines
ascending the up-draughts, dwindling
into the blue heaven, their chevrons
pointing towards that rock which lies
on the other side of hidden things.

In the Attic at Work

As I turn off the lights I feel
them sneak between the sensor beams,
passing through infrared, half-
remembered echoes in the rooms

which wink out one by one. They
are the revenants from the day's work,
the secrets let loose by the tongues
which stay for comfort in the dark

and dissipate like long-held breaths:
the baby bodies of themselves
that float on air or follow scents
down corridors where sense dissolves.

They flap like drowning fish, drag
their feet across the floor, persist
long after those who called them up
are gone and like a palimpsest

I read them just beneath the surface
of the ordinary air.
I call their names gently and place
a tick against the register.

This is my duty: closing up
the shop, alarming, putting to bed
these echoes, letting them exhale,
pulling sheets over their heads.

As I patrol the corridors
a meteor's descending flight
across a screensaver mirrors
the Leonids through an angled skylight.

A Nightjar

Goatsucker, puckeridge, poisoner-bird, lich-owl,
gabbleratch – these are the names of night-born fear
from far-flung farms and blind lane-ends – Fern Owl:
keep me safe with your wheeze at twilight; birch-black
drifter-between-copses, inoculate me with decoction
of feather, spore-of-the-glades, fragments of meteor;
let me walk under the dew-fall, hold in my traction
the Earth, fly open-mouthed through the mothy dark.